The Widow Whispers Grief

Natalie Brenson-Sangster

BookLeaf Publishing

India | USA | UK

Presentation by *BookLeaf Publishing*

Web: www.bookleafpub.com

E-mail: info@bookleafpub.com

ISBN: 9789358317268

First edition 2023

DEDICATION

To my beloved husband, Shawn, until we meet again.

ACKNOWLEDGEMENT

I acknowledge every soul that has felt grief and fought to survive the journey of healing from it.

PREFACE

Grief is part of life we cannot defer or avoid. If we love we will grieve, we will experience loss and the many moments of sorrow that come with it. Grief comes in stages, five to be exact, denial, anger, bargaining, depression and acceptance. In this small collection of poems I express my experience with the stages of grief in hopes of showing the reader that they are not alone in their grief journey and that you can survive the stages of grief.

The Widow Whispers

Please don't leave me was all that she could say
When they finally told her he had gone away
But she already knew for he had come to say
goodbye
She begged him to stay in the light knowing he
would try
But it was not meant to be for the Lord needed
him more
He took his hand out of hers and walked him to
the shore
There the angels waiting sang a song of love
He turned to see her crying and longed to lift
her up
She cried for the sudden loss of the love and ight
of her life
She cried that she is a widow now when
yesterday she was a wife
The tears fall like rain drops morning, noon and
night
She longs to get a sign from him that would turn
the dark to light
And in her darkest hour the widow whispers a
prayer for him to hear
Please don't leave me here alone please show me
you are near

A touch, a voice, a memory sweet will somehow
ease her pain
The widow whispers please come back through
tears that fall like rain
He tries so hard to let her know that he is there
and loves her still
The widow whispers into the dark I love you and
I always will

Widow Tears

A wife becomes a widow in a moment without a
choice
She finds herself in silence longing to hear his
voice
Her eyes well up with widow tears that differ
from the rest
For in these tears are the memories of the man
who knew her best
Widow tears will fall like rain full of sorrow
when she wakes
That he will not be beside her in the steps that
she must take
These tears will fall a hundred times throughout
the day ahead
For every memory that comes to mind and every
word he said
No regrets are left behind because they got it
right
Only sadness for the loss she feels every
morning and every night
She prays he will come to her in a dream so
vivid and so clear
And gently he will wipe away each and every
tear
In the dream he promises he will stay and wait

Until she comes to meet him there and reunite
their fate

If You See Him

If this message gets to Heaven can you pass it on
To the man I love the most and miss since he's
been gone
He's the one looking down, up there watching
over me
His smile will make the angels sing and set the
lonely free
He'll tell a joke with such a laugh, the sweetest
sound you'll hear
Could you tell him that I miss him and wish that
he was near
If you see him remind him that he will always
have my heart
and that my love lives on for him even though
we are apart.

Widow Down

The weight just became too much for her t
further bear
Not having him beside her, not feeling his
presence there
The nights of loneliness swallow her fragile
being whole
She cries out to the Lord above to help her
soothe her soul
Widow down in the quiet night the tears no
longer have a sound
She fears a life without him she is a widow
down
Waiting for the numb to finally fill her heart
So she can see another day and make another
start
She knows she must go on and somehow make it
through
She knows she is a widow down and she knows
what she must do
Find the strength she knows remains from the
man that she lost
And live the life she still has no matter what the
cost
He did not leave her here in vain for her to fade
away

She will go on with his memory to always light
her way

Grief Changes

They say that grief changes as each passing day
rolls on
It will come in ebbs and flows not staying quite
so long
But what they do not talk about is how it
changes you
Grief can change so much that you soon forget
what is true
It changes how you see the world and all the
beauty it should hold
It changes how you see yourself, now alone and
feeling old
Grief steals away the beauty that you once let
shine through
It casts a heavy shadow upon the shell that is
now you
Grief causes pain that shows so deep within your
tear filled eyes
The darkness that surrounds the skin your
makeup no longer hides
The cheeks are sunken in and withered skin
remains
The light you had has dimmed and your heart is
wrapped in chains

Yes grief changes many things, none of which
we have control
Grief will change you to your core and to your
very soul.

Within the Never

We loved well and for that there is no regret
We made our moments matter and I will not
forget
My sadness is so deep within and my heart is so
broken
But not because we left any words of love left
unspoken
My sorrow lies within the nevers that I am left to
face
Never again will we have a picnic at our special
place
Never will we laugh again at the things that we
found so funny
Never will we fish again on the river on day
warm and sunny
Never will we dance again heart to heart to our
favorite song
Never can you hold me close in your arms so
strong
Never will we get to dream of a future of us
together
All the precious opportunities now exist within
the never.

If I Hear Your Voice

If the wind blows by and touched my tear
stained cheek
I will turn my face towards the breeze even
when I'm weak
I'll listen for the wind to tell me what I hear
If I hear your voice within I will shed a joyful
tear
The days flow by one by one and the nights are
all the same
I listen with my heart and soul to hear you say
my name
I long to feel you next to me transcending space
and death
If I hear your gentle voice I'll gladly share my
breath
Just so you can stay with me even just a little
while
I'll give my strength all to you just to see your
timeless smile
I hope that you can hear me when aloud I say
your name
And tell you that I love you and I am thankful
that you came
Even in a moment you see I need your strength
and love

Please come back to be with me from your home
above

Please Be Patient

I am not sure of my footing since losing my rock
I am not sure of who I am with each tick of the
clock
Time keeps passing me by and you are gone
from my life
I don't know who I am now if I am not your wife
I struggle with my feelings and the tears still
easily fall
I forget I have made plans and I forget to return
a call
I miss appointments and deadlines, things just
slip my mind
I can't move past your absence and feeling left
behind
I hope others will be patient as I work through
this endless pain
Each memory we made together reminds me of
what will never be again
I hope they will be patient as I stumble and I fall
Or when I feel so frozen and can't break through
the wall
I hope they will be patient when I try to catch
my breath
Because it is so hard to breathe ever since you
left

Please be patient while I work out what I'm
supposed to feel
As I try to understand that losing you was so
real.

If I could

If I could see you just one more time I would
hold you a little longer
If I could hear you just one more time I would
be a little stronger
If I could have just one more day with you here
by my side
We would live, love and laugh so much until
happy tears were cried
The happy tears would flow so free and
gratefulness would grow
If I could have just one more day I would never
let you go.

I Couldn't Keep You

It took so long to find you after so many
heartaches and fallen tears
So afraid to try loving again but you took away
those fears
You came and showed me how to love the way it
was meant to be
How could it ever end with you being taken
away from me
I thought we'd have forever because we finally
found the one
In each other we found happiness our life had
just begun
But I couldn't keep you, you had to go away
No matter how I begged you, you knew you
couldn't stay
In a moment all the dreams we made became my
memories
Of the sweetest love I have ever known, it
brought me to my knees
But I couldn't keep you no matter how hard I
prayed
If my tears could have saved you, with me you
would have stayed.

Like the Tide

The grief is like the waves of the ocean, ebbing
and flowing through
It fills me up and takes my breath when I think
of you
Like the tide it rushes and quietly takes me down
It pulls me under , so confused with the darkness
all around
Then it weakens and I see the light, for a
moment I can breathe
Then the tide and tears flow in again, this is
what it is like to grieve
I am thankful for the love we shared and
memories that we made
I wish we had more time to love I wish you
could have stayed
But like the tide I will find my way and change
with every wave
The ground beneath me will shift and move, but
my love for you I'll save
Until we meet again my love, and your hand
returns to mine
I keep my heart open to you and pray you send a
sign
To tell me that you love me still and by my side
you'll be

Until the tide sweeps me out to where you wait
for me.

Talking With God

He was one of the good ones simply the very
best
You saw that he was special and my faith you
would test
You took him without warning and no chance to
say good bye
My heart shattered into pieces and all I could do
was cry
Why have you taken the one I love away from
me tonight
My world is so much darker now while you have
so much light
I know you are watching to see if my sadness
turns to rage
I will still believe you needed him as I turn
another page
I know you are not a God of spite and out to
break my soul
I know that you will comfort me and help my
heart heal whole
But if you could let him see how much I miss his
smile
Let him come to sit with me for a little while
Let me know he is close by so I can tell him how
I feel

Please let him touch me softly so I know that it
is real
I promise I will live a life that is full and his
memory I will keep
Please let him come to talk with me in my
dreams when I sleep

My |North Star

You always helped me find my way like a north star so true
Never did I feel misguided or unloved by you
So now that I am lost and feeling so unsure
I need your loving guidance like I did before
If you see me struggle from where you are above
Please send me the guiding light of your eternal love
For my love is steady and never will it blur
Please be my true north like you always were
Guide my path that lays before me as travel it alone
Help me learn to be alright again here on my own
I'll look for you at nightfall in the darkened sky
The brightest light that reaches out as my loving guide.

A Prayer for You

I miss your presence in my life, the sound of
your laughter fades away
I try to keep each memory alive and every night
I kneel to pray
I pray you're close and hear my prayer I whisper
in the night
I miss you my love and all we shared I hope
that you're alright
I pray you have peace and comfort in God's
heavenly home
I pray your loved ones met you there and that
you're not alone
If prayers could have kept you here by my side
forever
I would pray for just one more day of us being
here together
Leaving me here to miss you and knowing you
could not stay
So a prayer for you I will send from my heart to
you above
You will always be my light and my forever
love.

Just For Today

Today I am just going to sit and let myself be
broken
and sit in the sadness with no words spoken
Today I let the tears fall freely streaming down
my face
while I mourn your absence from this place
I will cry without an ounce of any shame
and into the sky I will call out your name
Today was a strange day I was not prepared to
face
Every piece of my shattered heart taking up
more space
Each of your dreams I watched taken away
Brought back the pain and heartbreak of that day
I feel like you see me and hear my words
I long for a sign from the red feathered bird
If one comes to call and sing me its song
I think I would have the strength to go on
But for today I am going to feel what I feel
and sit with the sadness and accept that it's real.

Who Am I

I knew who I was on that day when you kissed
me goodbye
I couldn't imagine a life without you, I couldn't
even try
I knew who I was when you left, I was your
loving wife
I lost my sense of who I am when you lost your
life
Who I am without you I truly do not know
They say I am a widow now, and onward I must
go
My love for you still flows through my broken
heart
No matter how far away you are we will never
be apart
You will always be the truest love of my tattered
life
Today they call me your widow, but I am still
your wife
We will dance to angels singing and Heaven will
rejoice
Until that day I see you I will make each day a
choice
To live my life to the fullest with you as my
guiding light

And I will tell you that I love you each and
every night

The Message

I have struggled and I've fallen since the Lord
called you home
I have searched for signs from Heaven when I
am feeling so alone
I have prayed for you to come to me on my
darkest night
You heard my wishes and sent to me a feather oh
so white
Your message told me you were here and that
your were at peace
And that you would stay with me until the waves
of sorrow cease
I felt your presence in my heart and it eased the
deepest pain
I saw the power of your spirit and heard you say
my name
Never will I doubt your presence and the
messages that you leave
Because my love has no boundaries within my
heart I do believe
My message for you is simple, forever you have
my love
I will send to you my sweetest dreams while you
wait for me above

Great Love

With great love comes great loss when that love
has to go away
With great loss comes great pain, it is the price
you pay
For happiness is the greatest gift just like the
greatest love
But it is only on loan to us from the Lord of
above
There will come a time this love is called back
from where it came
And you are left in misery and unrelenting pain
You think you will never breathe again the way
you did before
The crushing weight of loneliness fills your very
core
Then one day you they say you wake up with a
sense of calm
That the one you lost has been to see you and
they are never really gone
They live within your heart and all the memories
that you made
And though you cannot see them, close to your
side they've stayed
Every sunny morning and every moonlit night

They come to you within your dreams and there
they hold you tight

I heard You Say

I heard you speak to me as if it were a dream
Your voice was so clear to me like a heavenly
beam
You said it is time I tell you what you need to
know
About the day I had to leave and why I had to go
My story was written in the stars long before
that day
I met the Lord in the light, he said that I could
stay
He told me that it was my time but that I had a
choice
I listened to what he had to say and the kindness
in his voice
He said my son I see your struggle to leave
behind such love
I know you are unsure if you should join me
here above
But you see your heart is tired and it is time for
you to rest
I've prepared a place for you here with me, I
think it would be best
But I love your dearly so if you want to stay you
can

But your heart will still be tired, you'll be a
different man
Your limits will be challenging and make you
feel unwell
I love you as my child, so this truth to you I tell
I listened to him with my heart and I knew I had
to go
I asked if I could see you so that you would
always know
I love deeply from where I am as much I loved
you there
And now you know why I left and that I truly
care
I will always be beside you, just in a different
way
And now I have a sense of peace because of
what I heard you say.

In The Moon

Tonight the air seems clear and crisp
Fall's first gentle welcome kiss
The water glistens in the moon's soft light
I feel you here close to me on this autumn night
In the moon I see your smile
I know you've come to sit awhile
The glow that reaches out to me
Warm and soft like you used to be
In the moon I see our love
Still shining bright from above

Writing You Back to Life

Since the day you left this world for the one
where spirit lives
I have been lost in this world seeking signs that
spirit gives
My healing comes from signs and words I
search for everyday
A heart in the sky or a poem from my heart is
the surest way
I feel I am writing you back to life with every
word I write
and that you'll come to dry my tears in the still
of night
Even if you could come to me in a dream and
touch my soul
I would write my life away for yours to make
your spirit whole
To bring you back for another day so we could
all see your smile
and hold you close to each of us for a little while
So I will write and write some more hoping
magic will arise
and in spirit or in the flesh I will look into your
eyes.